MW01705139

MISSIONARY—THAT'S RIGHT

Missionary—That's Right

Written by Mark Weinrich

Illustrated by Brenda Wintermyer (Step One Design)

Missionary—That's Right is a story in the *Missionary—That's Me!* series

CHRISTIAN PUBLICATIONS / Camp Hill, Pennsylvania

Faithful, biblical publishing since 1883

Christian Publications
3825 Hartzdale Drive, Camp Hill, PA 17011

ISBN: 0-87509-559-3
Printed in the United States of America

95 96 97 98 99 5 4 3 2 1

When my brother Jeremy climbed on our school bus, he looked sad and mad—like he'd just had to eat broccoli.

I wondered why, but he wouldn't tell me.

When we got off the bus, he walked home with his head down, kicking pebbles down the sidewalk.

"What's wrong, Jeremy?" Mom asked when we got home.

"The kids in my class made fun of me," he said softly.

"Why did they do that?" she asked.

"Mrs. Waller asked all the kids what they want to be when they grow up," Jeremy replied. "When I said, 'I want to be a missionary,' the kids started teasing me and Mrs. Waller didn't say a thing. Last year Mrs. Gilbert thought it was neat that I wanted to be a missionary."

Big tears rolled down Jeremy's cheeks and Mom hugged him.

"I don't want to be a baseball or basketball player like the other kids. I want to be a missionary," Jeremy said.

"Well, there's nothing wrong with that," Mom said. "The other kids were wrong to make you feel bad about wanting to be a missionary."

Then she placed the cookie jar and two glasses of milk on the table. "After you eat your cookies, why don't we go out and do something fun together?" she asked.

Jeremy dunked a cookie in his milk and nodded.

"What will we do?" I asked.

"It's a surprise," Mom said. "But first we'll have to get rid of your milk mustaches."

Mom reached for her Bible and we headed for the car. "Let me show you a Bible verse," Mom said after we fastened our seat belts.

"In Mark 8:36 Jesus said, 'For what does it profit a man to gain the whole world and lose his soul?' "

"What does it mean?" Jeremy asked.

"It means that you and Jamie are VERY special people to God," Mom replied.

"You see," Mom continued, "your souls are worth more than all the world's wealth."

"Wow!" I said. But Jeremy said, "I still don't understand."

"Let's go on a mystery tour," Mom said. "I want to show you just how special you are."

"Will there be surprises?" Jeremy asked.

"You'll find out," Mom said as we pulled out of the driveway.

The first stop on our mystery tour was the bank.

As we sat outside the big building Mom asked, "Do you know what's in there?"

"Money," Jeremy said, "*lots* of money."

"That's right. But you know what? Your souls are worth more than all the money in this bank," Mom smiled and said.

"More than all the piles of money in the bank?" Jeremy exclaimed.

"Yes," Mom said, "and more than *all* the money in *all* the banks in *all* the world. Let's go to our second mystery tour stop and we'll see again just how special you are to Jesus."

FINE JEWELRY

Then Mom drove to the jewelry store, and we looked in the display window. The gold and silver jewelry sparkled in the shiny glass cases. I liked the diamonds best, and Jeremy liked the funny-looking watches.

"I can guess why you brought us here," Jeremy said. "Our souls are worth more than all the jewels in this store."

"And *all* the jewels in *all* the world," I added.

"Isn't it exciting to know how special you are to God?" Mom asked.

We smiled and nodded. And I wondered where the mystery tour would take us next.

Our third tour stop was the grocery store. *What are we doing here?* I thought.

We pushed our cart through the aisles, passing the fruit, vegetables, meats and candy until we came to the cereals.

"What are we doing here?" Jeremy whispered.

I just shrugged my shoulders and followed Mom down the aisle.

"We're not just going to shop, are we?" Jeremy asked.

"No," Mom said. Holding up a cereal box, she asked, "What do we do with cereal?"

"We eat it," I said.

"And play with the free toy and then throw the box away," Jeremy added.

Mom laughed. "That's right," she said. "Now hang onto your thoughts. We've got one more place to go."

As we drove to the fourth mystery tour stop, Mom said, "Think about the cereal box again."

"The full box or the empty box?" I asked.

"The empty one. What do we do with it?" Mom asked.

"After we use the cereal we throw the box away," Jeremy said.

"Some people live like that," Mom said. "Their lives are used up and thrown away. They don't even realize how much their lives are worth to Jesus."

"How sad," I said.

"Oh! I think I understand now," Jeremy replied. "Missionaries help people understand how much they're worth to Jesus."

GENERAL HOSPITAL

"You're right," Mom said as we drove into the hospital parking lot.

"This is our last stop on the mystery tour," Mom said, but she didn't have to ask any questions; we knew what happened in hospitals.

"This is where people help people," I said.

"Doctors and nurses work here," Jeremy added.

"Yes, you're both right," Mom said, "but doctors can only help people for a time. Missionaries help people now and forever when they tell them about Jesus and how He died for them."

GENERAL

"Wow," Jeremy exclaimed, "I really am special!"

"Yes, you are," Mom said, "and you want to do one of the greatest things that a person can do for God."

"No matter what the kids say now," Jeremy said, "I know I am going to do what God wants me to do. I want to help people understand how much they're worth to Jesus and that He loved them enough to die for them."

"That's wonderful, Jeremy," Mom said. "But there's one more thing you need to remember. . . ."

"When Jesus told us to go into all the world and preach the gospel He gave us a promise," she continued.

"What promise is that?" Jeremy asked.

"He said, 'I will be with you always.' "

"Even at school?" Jeremy questioned.

"Even at school," Mom replied. "And don't forget that Jesus will be with you when you serve Him one day as a missionary."

"Boy, are we special!" Jeremy exclaimed.

Mom smiled. "You sure are."

ABOUT THE AUTHOR

Mark Weinrich is the pastor of Fellowship Alliance Church. He and his wife, Lucy, live in Truth or Consequences, New Mexico with their children, Amie and Matthew. Mark is a prolific writer, having published more than 300 articles and poems in over 78 publications. He is the creator of the *Missionary—That's Me!* series and has written four books for the series. He is also the author of *The Light Chaser Mysteries,* a series for preteens with an underlying spiritual theme.

Hey Kids!

If you enjoyed *Missionary—That's Right*, why not read other books in the *Missionary—That's Me!* series: *Meet the Missionary*, *The Missionary Treasure*, *The Missing Missionary*, *The Waiting Missionary* and *I Want to Be a Missionary*. And if you enjoy reading stories about missions and missionaries, Christian Publications has two other series available for children: a series of missionary biographies entitled *The Junior Jaffray Collection of Missionary Stories*; and four books of true stories from mission fields around the world—*Bare, Beautiful Feet*, *A Happy Day for Ramona*, *The Pink and Green Church* and *The Potato Story*.